"Gopi Warrier's innate genius lies in synthesising world mythology, both Eastern and Western" - *The Hindustan Times.*

"Gopi Warrier's poems contain precise images of a coldly ranged occidental world, sterile and mechanical, almost soulless. In contrast are the many references to Karma, Guru, Ganapathy, Krishna and the Kundalini. He deals with both worlds with an "exactitude", all the time seeking harmony" - *Indian literature.*

LAMENT OF JC

Poems by Gopi Warrier

The Delhi London Poetry Foundation
150 West Cromwell Road London W14 9AD

Acknowledgements

Paintings
Cover painting - "Myth of Delos" by John Merton
Painting opening Part III "Heavenly Organ" by Adolf von Bernd
Painting opening Part I by Baldev Gambir from the poet's collection
Painting opening Part IV "Buddha" by Sarah Merton from the poet's collection
Painting by Phung from the poet's collection
Painting accompanying "The Lament of JC" by Rawlinson from the poet's collection

Illustrations by Amanda Brett

Printed by Leighton Printing

Photography by Harold Bennett

Typeset by Mrs K Jassal

Production Manager Miss A Herrero

Published April 1999
ISBN Number: 0 9535679 0 7

The Delhi London Poetry Foundation
150 West Cromwell Road
London W14 9AD

Dedicated
to
Mahaganapathy
Guru and Saviour

*"I break coconuts for Ganapathy in this final match,
to bowl Maya out, tired after her long innings
shuffling desparately at the crease"*

Introduction

Over the past 20 years, I have carried out research into the mysteries of Qumran and origins of Christian mythology. I have also had personal experience of many of the revelations contained in this book. One of the main principles that governs them is the law of Karma which says that we must bear the consequences of all actions, both good and bad. In Karma is a Slow Virus, written in the early 1980's, the advent of BSE or mad cow's disease was clearly foretold as were other mutations like HIV.

These poems scrape away the layers of ignorance deeply encrusted on the western(ised) soul. They are like great gulps of fresh air to a man in an airless room. The poem 'Lament of J.C.' may seem radical or even blasphemous, but it is part of a revelation that we are privileged to receive at the end of this millennium. The Jesus who laments today the disastrous turn of events after his feigned death and resurrection is overcome with remorse at the ensuing centuries of persecution of the Jews not to mention Muslims and Hindus.

This is a religion which, founded on a propagandist lie has exhausted its appeal in the West but which is still being exported to 'untouched' areas of the world where converts can be bought for a few rupees or a square meal to feed the AD 2000 marketing targets of its rabid right wing evangelists.

So this poem offers an opportunity for true seekers who are Christians, to be released from the arrogant dogma that the path to God is only through one man, to humbly realise that he was only one of several prophets who received teachings from Hindu mystics.

Then they can really begin to learn from other sacred spiritual cultures much older and wiser than theirs which for years they have been forced to distrust and deride.

Hinduism tells us that we are now in the last stages of the dissolution of the Universe where Maya or the illusion of the manifest world must be seen through and man must turn toward a spiritual journey leading to reunion with God. If the human condition, as described so chillingly in a song for the Millennium, is to be transcended, then we need to read between the lines of these poems and seek their source.

DAVID DOUGLAS CHRISTOPHER McALPINE
Author of "CruciFiction - The Hoax of Christianity"

Contents

Part I - The Past

Part II - The Present

The Bookseller

Poets

Feminist

An Aquarian Physiotherapist

From Exmoor to Porlock Hill

In Dying is a Culture

The Buddha of The Suffering

In Praise of The English

Part III - The Future

A Song for The Millennium

Writing a Poem

Indian Afternoon

Hindu Analyst

Insignificance

Kundalini

Superstring

Taurus

At a Carnatic Music Concert in Madras

The Breath of The Shining Skull

R.E.M.

Gemini London

The Philosophy of The Googly

Ganapathy Loves Cricket

Cricket at Lords

Priest Striding Towards Heathrow

Into Priesthood

Destruction of Tripura

Part IV - The Eternal

After The Storm

Kaliyamardan

From Void

The Marriage of Lord Venkateswara

And Padmavati

PART I

The Past

"For so long, so long
je te connais
la
tristesse"

Ezra Pound

Karma is a Slow Virus

Like a mole, an unpleasant looking wart
Karma is a slow virus
encrusted on the soul of man.

'Kuru' and 'Crutzfeld-Jacob'
may take twenty years to manifest,
my poor sister-in-law, a pathologist in New Orleans
dreads the thought.
Karma has no known incubation period,
could take lifetimes before it dawns as dark
terror in the afternoon of a life
that didn't seem to deserve such sorrow.

Is Karma infectious? Yes, an opportunistic
one that emerges when one's stock
of good, like immunity, has been
exhausted over many lives.
Then even the mere kiss, the straw
of an ingratitude can ignite the flame of torture,
leaving the mind seeking death
over life. Not even the funeral
pyre or the grave has enough interferon

to kill this virus. Invisible, safe
in some intercoastal muscle of the soul
it burrows on till the light
of the spirit dawns.

Swastika

In this Bavarian air an electric
crackling of danger.
Here in the woods the mother was
shot or shot herself. The daughter had to bend
forward to be taken (they said willingly)
in the rear. A military
truck, red lights subdued,
reverses into my dream.

We were Aryans
with the viral energy of Gods.
We arrived here as dust on the edges
of light from over a million exploding
Supernovae. Particles of brightness, which like charms
had the clarity of God's kingdom though
in its soft underside our alter-ego desired separation if
not freedom. Mutation of the protozoid
inhabitation in nature and its self-destruction was our stated goal.
For they were Aborigines,
demonic races who fell with Lucifer.

But in liberation nature
herself changed, her own image no longer immune.
Light's distortion
penetrated her cellular core, broke
the mirror of her pure waters.
Now only the stench remains, the semen
rotting in plastic sheaths, wombs
of a new generation.

In a red sky black letters,
occult signs, spell magic and evil-
the self detonation of nature by her own
left hand. She will, as intended, have to invite
dissolution, uterus emptying
into the black hole of planetary collapse.
Is benediction a pure white snake, rising
from the gloom of a lost species,
a civilisation floundering for over ten thousand years?

Oh Bavaria, how I remember thee
second receptacle for the fallen
soul.

The Punishment

As he slept,
at one in the night,
the blue van drew up

in quiet menace.
Three large men
in red anoraks came out from the back.
As the flag flew
the colours merged
red, blue and their own.
Then after a click of heels
and a smart salute
they disappeared.
But he knew they were still there.
Still in his street.

Was this his punishment from Zacariah
for not telling the truth
last time around?

A U-Turn at Hanover Terrace

At Hanover Terrace, in Regent's Park,
my driver makes a sharp U-turn in a black Mercedes.
A blonde in her late-forties in a BMW, Luftwaffe powered
applies a sudden brake to avoid us
and is hit from behind by a Moroccan looking man
driving a battered old car. He argues
with her and drives away without giving the sorry
details of his existence for which he prays
at the Park's giant mosque, copperdome sun-gathering in winter.

This is the junction where
I have lived before and may live again.

I wonder if this was the end of a karma which ended with
Kristallnacht
after the crusades and a crucifixion made to look like death
but led instead to a life of peace in Kashmir.

Six million Jews were killed, Temples and Mosques razed,
countries colonised and raped on the moral strength
of a lie of death and resurrection.

I am guilty but get away with only an hour's detention
in Nuremberg on mistaken identity.
The man whose head was sliced and put upon a platter
rots away in a Paris jail.

I lied but he spoke the truth.

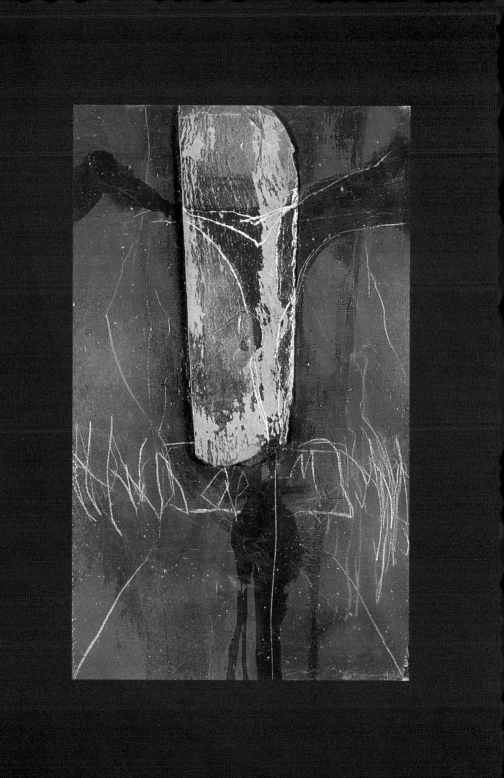

The Lament of J C

After four hours on the Cross,
I fall, as planned, still conscious.
Magdalena now M
tends me with sensual care, taking part,
as she always did, in that ultimate deception.

She applies commiphora to my bleeding wounds
and covers my face with her voluptous body so that
none would see my gratitude. The Roman soldiers
look at her contemptuously with lust.

I think, in opiated daze, of
how badly I have treated her.
How I cursed and rebuked her for the pleasure
she took from men from whom she took money to feed me.
My jealousy at her encounters was sharp
and pitiless though I depended on them.
Her residual longing for shopkeepers
and other men of petty means when she is now
a princess once baffled me - but that
was how she fed us all then, though
she and I kept the others guessing.

It was a relief not to die
and fun to play the game of miracles.
I blessed Magdalena that all she wished
and prayed for would come true.

Here I am now using her prayers
as I did her body once, for love and sustenance.

I never thought that the Cross
will one day become an icon
of torture and oppression to spell
the death of a culture that helped me
live through the crucifixion, and then
received me and protected us for 50 years.

That the mantras I learnt at the feet
of the Nath masters with which I meditated on the cross
will be reviled
by missionaries bearing my name. That
the mountains that gave me refuge
will be torn apart along a line drawn
by a drunken British General in a fit of pique.
That six million will be killed
for the crime of killing me who never died.
I taught forgiveness and claimed resurrection.
Ha! I cannot but laugh in self-contempt
at those monstrous lies I helped create.

From each Jew I see I seek forgiveness
with each breath I fight the myth
from whose retaliating karma forms my stigmata.
In Germany my soul shudders with electric fright
at a darkness I comprehend as the evil from my own untruth.

Cardinals, Archbishops and Popes hand
in hand with the C.I.A. now re-market me as Che,
not believing a fig, my story.
Unlike the fig tree that I so intemperately
cursed, these pompous men stand as accursed
as the bankers who deny the poor.

Their call is to
evangelise the heathen but collect money
for their own nest eggs, mistresses
or if nothing else for the wives'
varicose veins operations to be done privately,
not with plebs on the NHS.
These are the grand missions of their petty lives
and they must of course look
good on the television, each parish church a snake -pit
of egos and class pretence.

There are other, more deserving folk
where my people once reached.

Thomas whom I had despatched
to the green paradise of Kerala
carried on rough seas by dhows from Persian gulf
died last year in Madras. Thirty two years ago I blooded
him in St. Thomas Mount where Mrs Morgan
initiated us into the pleasures all men seek.
He converted the Brahmins
in Kerala by throwing up the water of their morning
prayer, the Gayathri, invocation of the light.
Like a whiff of smoke,
the water went up but never came down
and they converted bearing my name
but neither poor Thomas nor the Brahmins knew
that this siddhi I learnt from
the Brahmins themselves 20 years before
in distant Orissa at the Temple of Jagannath
from the Chief Priest for Krishna, Subhadra and Balarama,

the trio that reappears
in varied forms, intent only on their war on evil.

Poor Thomas died last year of a broken heart,
as have all the others, burnt out
by quick success like the barrow boys
in a trading room.
Their Ferraris were churches, elaborate costumes and
the myths around their name
all tutored in marketing at the business schools
of Qumran.

Pesharim played tricks with their memories
and the truth as they twisted each mundane fact
into myth and miracle to make me
the Son of God.
(I am sad, guilty and ashamed).

They now make me Che
Tomorrow I will be Thatcher,
Anglo-Saxon Goddess of the Night.
They have changed my sex. My cross is
now an egg, then a candle.
It will soon become a penis
the linga of Shiva, at least the final truth.

I did not cry
The curtains of the temple did not tear
from top to bottom.
They did not tear at all.

....cont

But I do now roar
like the thunderbolt of Indra
armed with the trident of Shiva
Aghora and the Sudarsana.
These missiles must and
will be launched if the charade does not
stop, if the Satan of the West
keeps using my name to put their
greedy and rapacious hands on cultures
where there are still sacred truths,
where real Gods and Goddesses still
play and manifest their power.
I have become one with them.
I do not know my face, but I know
the armour that I wear.

Taking Breaths
(For my father)

I didn't often think of you.
But this summer, few months
before you died
an ordinary
medicated shampoo reminded
me of you.

Clean, strong yet vulnerable.

That unique smell of an asthmatic's inhaler
and air-conditioned office room
where you exercised a government's
power.

A major accident kills hundreds
on that famous line you built forty years ago.

Then you die alone, clutching
the inhaler in your hand.

Knowing's Pain

As she is wheeled into the surgery
She asks meekly,
voice weak with exhaustion -
"Is this Black Magic?"

I know what it is
but I cannot talk,
having known all along
that this will happen.

When he cannot intervene,
stop an act that conjoins three
inevitable paths - past,
present and future - an astrologer's heart
is nailed by it's own knowledge.

Pain

Pregnant woman
bending over paddy
smiles
knowing her child's first breath
will be of fresh hay.
Not for her the starched linen
or sterile steel

in hospitals. Pethidine
will never flow in
her veins
whose thresholds of pain

are barricaded. Her thoughts moored
to that single event
she will first take
her husband's praise
and then the pleasure of her child.

Hemicrania

The Greeks called you
the onesided monster -
powerless like a demon princess to occupy
at any time more than one
hemisphere of the brain.

You now try, like Parvati
to capture the other side of Shiva.

Even pain seeks completion.

Interviewing a Brahmin

An old tweed coat,
patched in places,
hung loose about his shoulders.
Over town collars and down his throat,
sweat trickled.
But it was the white stubble on his chin that ripped
my non-chalant facade
with edges shaper than of blades
he saved
each precious paisa for one meal a day -
that kept him walking.

At forty, with a wife and two sons in Bangalore
he walked the city street,
searching.
Neither Sanskrit,
his knowledge of the Vedas
nor his sacred thread
had helped him keep his job -
selling cloth,
last twenty years,
nor find another.

In his blood-shot eyes I saw
the dusty by-lanes he had trekked
cloth pieces in hand,
cheap rupee-a-bed hotels,
his proprietor's greed
lashing him on
and now the mist of hope.

How could I ever tell him
that this job was meant
only for 'convent educated' young men
with longish hair and accent
whose broad ties alone will sell products
to shopkeepers of a nation still in awe
of an old ruler's speech and dress?

Indian Socialites

Three hundred socialites waiting to be interviewed
three hundred million human beings waiting for a meal.

This 'contemporary couple' once boasted of imported cars and hi-fis.
Attended clubs and
balls
where they danced
to music they did not quite understand.

Now they subtly drop the name
of Yves St. Laurent,
mention friends on the continent
and talk pidgin French.
Passe, come couchez avec moi etc.

Their only claim to fame is the photograph
with a young leader.
The husband's advertising budget,
scotch,
and the wife's exposed navel does the rest,
buying fame in pages.

Three hundred socialites waiting to be interviewed
three hundred million human beings waiting for a meal.

Three Travellers

While others
sped towards the mirage
in limousines,
three travellers -
one world-weary,
one committed
and the other full of hope,
they - walked
in the direction of the promised land,
where grass was magic green
and dark blue lagoons
like a flighted ball
caught the spirit off-guard.
This land, between earth and paradise
was formed on a rare vapour.
Only the tested soul could pass.

They fought the heat,
the relentlessly burning sand,
digging deep for water.
Each animal they killed they ate
with a relish that may have shocked them earlier.

They celebrated their victories
and in the villages that dot the desert fringe,
became legend and folklore.

They established an ephemeral rule
over these settlements,
a network of power derived from victory
over nature, demarcating
their boundaries of pleasure from the desert
and sand
in food and wine
and in large eyes imploring from little huts
"Please belong".

Their route beyond the villages
now leads only into the desert
not the ethereal land they sought
to organise'.
Triumph of mirage.

Sudbury Town

She said she was going to Sudbury Town, I know
There are no buses to this place.
Or tubes.
Yet she went.

She has an old friend who lives
In Sudbury Town,
A woman who teaches English
To Asian children.
The children call her name
In tongues unused to English names.
They run behind her, pulling her saree,
Which she wears with love,
Though awkwardly.

She feels happier in Sudbury town
With this woman
And her hyperactive Punjabi kids.
I known she would like to live in Sudbury Town,
A fairy tale town.

Away from analysis,
From rooms with threatening inkblots
And a world which emphasises night and magic
To hers
That seeks childhood, light.

Maybe one day I will find that ordinary people live there.

And the bus,
Or the tube,
Which goes to Sudbury Town.

Saviours

In this zero-hour of the city,
when the moon refuses to shine
when I stand beside
the widowed sea
soliciting suicide from me
they come to me,
the galley slaves,
riding the blue.

PART II

The Present

"Parvati domesticates Shiva.
Kali provokes, angers and finally threatens him.
This is the natural progression of female energy"

Adi Shankara

Daughter of the Mountain

The Beginning of Kali

The Play with Kali

The Threat of Kali

The Retaliation of Kali

The Defeat of Kali and the Secret of Chidambaram

The Beginning of Kali

Deep within the indestructible
self's
powerful diamond core
nothing exists other than
pure light
and though nothing enters there
alone you have reached my soul.

The past is a mercurial flow into the present.
The lives we lived before
fall into and softly fill the crevices between us.
Pain explains itself in this mirror -
perfect reflection of the past.

I do not understand time as you do.
For me it is always still.
You define it, thereby extend
the corners of the universe
and my spatial interjection into void, creates,
each time,
the new reality.

No accidental act
each meeting tracing back past connections
finally consumed in your sensuality -
as a slim golden chain
sharp, curling serpent like,
pierces the green geode of true consciousness.
Primordial stone,
igniting 'kleem', tantric bijamantra of union,
ah! how precise the sukshma tantra of ordained reunion.

You are energy, the steel horse
moulded in the hot womb of June
neglected when born, as the sun
traversed the opposite pole in December.

The sagittarian fire awakens the serpent
and keeps spurring me,
who am air and spirit,
into the most dangerous of actions.

You once again become ancient Sendivogius
and with your hands
in a magical trance
reverse the Germanic Swastika.
Atharvana and Advaita samskaras fuse into one -
the cosmic force.

The Play with Kali

Of your lost kingdom
I knew nothing
except that your people
were of unusual warmth,
loved music and laughter
that the country's Libran love of harmony reached
a crescendo of sound
in the crepescular squares of Salzburg.
Far away, by your "seat" in Vienna
the quiet music of the Danube became
gentle witness,
accessory to secret yet
noble passions.
I knew also of your fine little horses
the Lippizaner, most suitable for dressage
whose sleek shanks
are more than matched
by your sagittarian rear
sensuously curving into golden thigh,
amazing evidence
of the Zodiac's architecture.
Was the hand of the sculptor
from Khajuraho
even there?
Your sense of daring
could startle a weak lover.
The proverbial Hapzburg wildness
ripples
like the reflection of fire
upon an armour of poise

silken elegance
and pearl-ringed neck.

Fire is your element,
true blue flame
from the mellowness of a candle that lights you gently
to your weakness for arson,
by a silver tongued Romeo
who lights the fuse
of dangerous passion and
in abuse, makes you fly, body arched in trust,
moth-like, unaware,
into sublime merger, the synthesis by fire.

Eyes intense, innocent of guile
you become Juliet and
in medieval, dim-lit rooms
where others dance and gorge themselves on food and drink
you seek love
in the most audacious fashion.

The Threat of Kali

Daughter of the mountain,
I see evil in your eyes,
the darkness of your sex,
the threat of death.

Against the dying sun
my plane from Salzburg descends
into the dark, menacing side of Tyrolean Alps.

I have never known you or anyone
else in Tyrol.
But just as I feared, you are at the airport gate,
waiting patiently. I cannot escape this fate,
for your gargantuan body hides the city of Innsbruck.
In your hand you hold the yellow flowers
you picked from the mountain sides for me.

Are you just a mountain girl, will you hug me to your breasts,
is your smile clear or is it the edge
of a knife from which blood will drip
on an old Hapzburg grave in Tyrol.

The Retaliation of Kali
(To my wife in intensive care)

Daughter of the mountain,
I see the incredible sweetness
in your eyes,
the whisper in your tired lips and
even in this anaesthetised agony
the light in your smile.

This event that I knew so
well, that haunted me for fifteen
years, has now come true. I see why
astrologers, miracle workers or even semi-
gods cannot play at being God
in the real operating theatre. Despite
the knowledge
I could do
nothing to avoid or ease your pain.

Seven different tubes run into you.
Under a white cloth, shoulders and
left breast exposed you lie
with the ventilator pumping hard, looking
more beautiful than ever before.
Your heart-rate is high but constant,
B.P. low, the temperature above
normal, the wound still bled.

This is no herbal medicine.
Occidental precision has taken over.
It is the quite, efficient murmur, the mantra
of the life support system that now keeps you
alive. Here science moves almost as gently,
as carefully as God.

But science cannot reach the part
that God can. From somewhere deep within that
ocean of your sleeping mind you hear
my voice. Though clinically unconscious
I see you eyes flicker inside
the closed lids with great effort, like a little
conscientious girl waking up late for school,
as though you've had enough rest and must now
get back to keeping me
going. Unnoticed by anyone else I see that tremor,
an infinitesimal flutter, run through your body. That
flicker of your selflessness
completely shreds my heart.

Now you lie there satisfied,
wounded like a little dog
that protected its master's life,
secretly smiling to yourself
at the knowledge that you took on
your right flank the torture, the knife
meant for me.

The Defeat of Kali and
the Secret of Chidambaram

Hawking hypes black holes and baby
universes, Einstein dances
puzzled over the embers of theories
still not unified.

They both ill treat the women who gave
them such love and care. Nor do they
or their fellow dons of European middle class
vintage penetrate the black hole
of their own illusions.

The "secret" simply glows,
its golden threads luminescent,
a harp latent with eternal mantras, all flowing
into pranava, the breath sound of the cosmos.
Galaxies, black holes and neutron stars form dew
drops on these kundalini strings
evaporating into cosmic sound.

Here is where Shiva defeated Kali in High Tandava
and then limited her destructive power.
He then went on to destroy the world himself
carving all but the prime soul
for a more auspicious creation.
Kali stands beside him in mute surrender.

My darling Kali, your tender love
is insecure like a child's.
Your flesh is weak. You crunch
and devour men in the black hole between your thighs.

Why do Hindu artists so wrongly draw you
with an old, haggard face and protruding tongue when
the remnants of your beauty are still in your ageing face
and proud breasts? And as we play and dance
the world burns down to cinder.
Only Maya dies.

Forty

I become forty with a bang.

First my wife nearly dies
and is saved
only by sudden, major surgery at 12
midnight, for a strangulated, gangrenous
bowel.

Then my father dies.

It takes 18 inches of my wife's bowel,
one for every year
to make me a man.

Shakti

In the Aquarian age
Gemini, the child
is sage, father to Libra.
And it's Libra that pushes the world painfully
into the Aquarian age. Thus the air trinity conjugates
a cyclical page.

But Libra is the soul's evolution
from Virgo. Soul memories
of the work ethic, need for precision
linger on.
So does the translucent virgin remain
in your clear eyes, in the softness
of your lips.
Virginal youth sculpts and moulds
your breasts so pointed,
their peaks firmly, knife-like
cuts a lover's lips, bruises his soul.

And like a Virgo,
You want concrete
proposals, nothing vague!
Fool, who can remain
concrete against the light,
the haze of such amazing grace.
That corresponds
to a firmness, a trace
of a Devata-like knowledge
in the edge of your laughter.
To secret syllables in your sound.
In that strength lies our past
and our shared future.

Pale Europe leaves the spirit
cold, misdirects the soul to a delusion
of ego's grandeur.
Yet, as we learn in the East
all men are gods,
women goddesses in love,
in true awareness.

Between your slender,
sensual thighs
O Devi, Goddess Shakti,
the warm, brown vastness of space.
In the face of such awesome beauty
Shiva
hesitates. Should he, lips bruised,
pleasure Devi or enter, subjugate
his power, thus create
yet another universe?

To a Travelling Libran

Outside the hotel the warm
blue sea.
Bombay's heat bruises
Your delicate skin that needs
gentler attention.
Dark glasses hide
your lustrous eyes and the silk blouse
the sculptured shape of desire.
Your clothes cling to your breasts and hips, true
beauty has no camouflage.
That you are Libran is reassuring -
a little cloud of rain
never idle, refreshing the barren
sky of Bombay.
You had such style in a simple
dress.
We haven't met in four
years now, but I still return
to your responsive smile,
it's warmth
and the knowledge in your eyes
of a spiritual kinship.

Pre-Natal

Having received the seed
half in passion,
half in a woman's unique, peculiar joy
of acceptance,
it brewed. Like a storm
it raged within her, took part
of her away. It changed
her internal landscape, rivers
swollen and flowing, rhythms
absorbed in a new sound.

She became hungry and primitive.
A goddess demanding, devouring
love. Then in a surge of wind
pain and blood she gave birth, the power
of prakriti alone.

Cough

Outside
The mist melts like a water colour.
In mid-February visibility is low and few
planes touch down at Delhi after
dark or early morning.

The twelfth floor of the Sheraton
in any city is a vantage
point. The hotel, at 2am, just drifting
to sleep, is an hour
or two behind the city, freezing
this late winter night. Air crew come
and go, in sleek uniforms,
at ungodly hours.

Down below, in the dust -
brown hutments of poor
workers, a woman coughs. Huddled
in an old blanket, her husband coughs
louder, only this time
the phlegm rattles. A sadder cough,
with the trace of emphysema or perhaps
T.B., a cartpuller's occupational hazard.

Voices carry in the desert night and
coughs, like yawns, are
infectious, replicated. In the next room the fat
businessman who had earlier walked
down the corridor from the health club in a bath towel,
also coughs, now
a smoker's cough.
The sixty Dunhill cigarettes he smokes
a day would, in Indian rupees, keep
a family clothed and fed for at least a month.

In my room, through the softness
of her silk saree, I choke on the sweet
nipple of an air hostess, preparing for take-off
to seventh heaven.

Autumn on the Hills of Jouy-en-Josas

Denuded branches,
Mellow sun,
After-noon's inexactitude.

Though la Vierge, in gothic flamboyant,
Says toujours interdit
Art grows.
The observatory predicts a painless day
That mind will step aside
To let the light pass
In the other direction.

Silent spider,
Your silver web
Splits,
Curls
And melts
Into the brown shores of autumn.

Condensing on a window pane
Is my summer's transparencies
Delaunay's magic circles,
Rude gentleness of a dark haired man
Smoking Gitanes.

Jouy-en-Josas is close to the chateau near Versailles where H.E.C
(Ecoles des Hautes Etudes Commerciale) is located.-

Academie Francaise

Even the intellectual French
hate the Arabs
whose dark charm defeats Gallic guile
in courtship.

The rare French blonde, like Le Pen's
wife prefers Arab passion to
French hypochondria.

This paranoia,
C'est normal, par ce que
La France est mort si
Joan of Arc eloped to Tunis.

Night Bus from Wall Street

In the night bus from Wall Street
are poems within poems.
Like this one
which was "kicked
out of the bus for it's nakedness,
but got on again at the next stop,
this time in a grey business suit,
copy of the Times under it's arm".

In the bus at 10.15
women are expectant.
Dressed in long skirts
they carry flowers. Their voices
do not echo the scream
of New York.

This one carried a sculpture.
I stare,
see it's green legs of clay
over her own -
warm, brown haired.
It's head is covered by a paper hood
reaching her chin. Polaroids submerged in hair
she looks up and feeling shy
under such examination
covers her face with the hood.

The bus driver believes
that Jesus will come again to Wall Street
and driving slow delivers
his sermon from the wheel.

Lithe bodies curving,
swimming into night,
New York forever
moving in a river,
the filtering of desire from laughter.

Nato

Arms for Nato
alms for the third world.

Bombs for Nato
Buns for the rest.

U.S. Foreign Policy

Today's puppet
Tomorrow's monster.

Today's arms buyer
Tomorrow's dictator.

Today's demon
Tomorrow's ally.

Wag the Dog

Air Supremacy is a psychopath
pilot, protected by his computer jet
decimating an ancient city.

Air Supremacy means the amputation
of childrens legs, women's breasts.

Air Supremacy is the dropping of
500 tons of bombs on nursery schools,
mosques and hospitals.

Air Supremacy means a pale, colourless
politician going up in the polls in
recently 'civilised' democracies.

Air Supremacy means the power
of a coward nation to bomb
brave foot soldiers.

The Bookseller

Unlike the wine seller
of the Rubaiyat they love
their books more
than the authors or readers and part
with them only in sorrow.

A dowry in reverse, the price
paid is for the cost of it's departure.

Poets

They see all
flying high
none to tend
their sores, their dripping
wounds. Flying
high and proud but terribly
alone.

In flight they nod
to other passing birds.
If and when they alight
(as they must), wings tired, souls thirsting
the company of other
birds or humans they chatter
loud and make peculiar noises,
chirping, crowing, screeching. Then scratching
they proceed to peck each others
feathers out but never the hearts
as humans do.
The lesser plume the better
for a certain kind
of flight.

Wounded more they fly.
They nod again at each other
in flight. Still friendly,
wiser for the fight.

Only the eagle flies
and dies alone.

Feminist

She wears her B.A.
in psychology like a pendant
between her small breasts.
If she had had a PhD
or larger breasts she might have
been less of a feminist.
After all, Clarissa next door,
after her boob operation is no longer a feminist.
Women with large breasts confuse her.
They seem to have a key
that so easily articulates a man's secret
dream.

Since they met, her poor,
tortured boyfriend has undergone a sea
change. She claims his sensitivity is only
an antenna that picks up entertainment whereas
hers is of an 'earth mother'. She says she hears
even the flutter of a bird in pain. Thus she cackles on.
He now prefers Spain in male company
and is half-impotent.

As earth mother she dabbled in Alexander
Technique, Tai chi and Zone
Therapy. She then 'moved on',
as they all do, to Buddhism but found
meditation too male dominated.

She has now graduated to witchcraft,
her most natural vocation.

An Aquarian Physiotherapist

Your gentle hands
expertly knead the shoulders and the neck,
like soft white foam rushing to quench
the flames of pain.
From this vantage point,
looking at your feet
the patient cannot see your mascara-less eyes
any longer. But he will assure you,
they are as beautiful this morning as any other.
Your voice has no trace of Singapore
or other exotic places where your father and the Navy went
and like a silken stream along the English country-side
undulates with each movement of your sensuous yet
gentle body, as you bend over, talking to the crippled
or those in pain.

Pre-occupied with your own need to evolve,
you don't respond
to strange places, strange people.
Your caution, concern for accuracy
the simple way you cost the pounds and the pence
for your services is touchingly sincere.

....cont

Jane Shattock, how soft yet firm,
there is no talk at all
of the longer term or a need to belong.
Like all Aquarians
you combine business
with the dispensation of grace
and your healing touch.
The clock strikes twelve
the time is done
you keep smiling for the next one.

From Exmoor to Porlock Hill

The bleakness of this heathen land
is no prosaic tragedy,
not recession nor material want -
post - Arthurian spiritual pall?

The knowledge haunts
that somewhere on this land
an occult presence demands
encounter with self
in truth
or
in evil.

Like the painting of some old soul
the moorland obeys
a command of silence,
eerie stillness
of sheep, bush and grass.
All movement is transgression,
alien acts,
emphasising transience.

Men in Porlock
have a sombre look,
cultivated air,
play country hosts.
Eyes not entirely in focus,
impatient with their day,
they await the call.

In Dying is a Culture

Poor Dhangopal Mukherjee
you lived uncared for in New York
probably bankrupt
almost certainly insane.

Even your name
that implied meditation on Krishna
has a ring of tragedy.

You were too much an Indian
to have left India.
Like Medusa
her Capricornian clutches
kept pulling you back
then spitting out
your heart.

Because you cared,
oozed pain
for Calcutta.
Didn't you know
that India often shoots
or wounds
those who madly love her?

Dear Dhangopal,
you should have known
that Death is not the same in India.
Kala is not New York's
possessive archangel
nor a devious Lucifer
waiting to steal your soul.
He is a lazy old
Indian peasant
who must sow you back next season.

Dhangopal Mukherjee was a poet from Calcutta who left India in the early twenties, wandered abroad and finally committed suicide in New York.

The Buddha of the Suffering

for David McAlpine

The last summer was fated,
the crucible. It brewed
disaster. When you came seeking
herbal remedies and the Buddha
in India, mother said you are
like another Buddha, innocent
of suffering, vulnerable, sincere. That one day,
without doubt, you will reach
your goal.

Though I would rather have
sent you alone to Bodhgaya
to receive the few inevitable knocks,
father said, no, this boy is our guest,
your colleague, we must protect
him in the lawless jungles of Moghulsarai -
crossroad for the old moghul chariot
path from Delhi, now
a railway town.

You were probably better
off, without the official jeep that broke
down, the government inspector
who gave you a military style
inspection of Benares and the bathing ghats.

Then, on the last day
in Bodhgaya you miss your water
flask and drink the local
brew. You see the Buddha, not in the
temple, but in agony, sitting in the loo
of an old guest house.

In Praise of the English

Whatever the faults of Brits
they make loyal friends
have great courage and are originals -
not replays of some American dream.
They win their wars.

The love of an English rose is gentle,
yet wildly sensual. In betrayal
is jealous rage. Her breasts are soft
and her heart responds to tenderness.

A well-bred Englishman will give
his life and even go to prison
for you. For him the difference between Eton
and Wormwood scrubs is marginal
as for a school of tramps moving
from one garden square to another in London.

But it is difficult to penetrate an English heart
so caught up in posturing and in such undue
loyalty to that old bat in Sandringham
and her spoilt brats who suck the blood
of deference from this nation.
The charade of divine right and fading pomp
keeps the loyalty of this nation so narrowly
between the seas of a no longer sceptred isle.

The English spirit will no longer fly
unless its mascot dies
a natural death like any other soap opera
from public boredom.

England does not need a King
when every English home is a castle.
England needs no Queen when every English woman
demands the devotion of Queens.

The poor and the lower class have the heart
and the art to reunite this nation, but
its blood must flow through republican veins
not tainted Saxburg-Gotha ones.

Opinion polls don't tell the truth.

PART III

The Future

Forgive me for the arrogance of thinking I am you
even though I am you.

A Song for the Millennium
(An elementary guide to the human condition)

Let in the fog, let in the fog
life is just a foot in the bog
let the drifting mist and the wind jog
your memories of unrequited love.

Let in the rain, let in the rain,
in your heart is unending pain
in transitory moments of joy why feign
true happiness that has always eluded you.

Let in the wind, let in the wind,
you have repeatedly lied and sinned
against the girl or boy who
gave you love and pinned
all their life's hopes on you.

Let in the fire, let in the fire,
whether you be a Queen, Prince,
Lord or Sire,
your final destination is the funeral pyre,
into which death's henchmen
will contemptuously hurl in your
corpse no longer you.

Let in the light, let in the light,
your soul is in the 13th,
the last day of it's flight,
is it day or is it the night
are these hell-fires burning bright
or are they satellite televisions still
taunting you?

Let in the dust, let in the dust,
Your soul's memories are turning to rust
you will soon incarnate due to
some creatures love or lust,
As man, animal or insect in a womb
meant just exactly for you.

Writing a Poem

Like a stranger, unannounced
you rang my bell.

I didn't know your face, your colour,
your hair, yet you came knocking
at my door and
I had to let you into the house,
into my head.

You then rearranged
the furniture, hung
some new paintings and left
quicker than I thought you would.

The house still looks the same.
But feels cleaner.

Indian Afternoon

Afternoon shimmers
Light
energy
saps
mutates into heat -
like a sharp knife flying.
Brown sand
vast space
make slices of digestible time.
Measured bits crumble into days
minutes and seconds.

In the east heat evens out.
Each second is like another.
Action seems meaningless -
other than an upward, outward move
from this giant bowl of sweat.

Everyone has a saint in him.
But the brave one meditates on his navel -
the end of the Fibre-optic cable
from the cosmic womb helps him
watch,
listen to eternity.
Its seventh whorl
holds the secret mantra
where time converts back into heat, light, energy.

Hindu Analyst
To Hari Singhal

You carry the smell of Southall with
you - the coffee stains, Indian spices.

When you tell me of your youth,
your father's shop and
of life in a gully where sewage
and water slushed through in the monsoon
I feel terribly sad - that you lived
thus and talk about it so readily.

On Vijaydashmi day
you do a puja for your computer.

As you tell me of the woman who at a local
temple, in a trance becomes Hanuman and guides
you to a hillside for a herb
to cure your asthma, I see you for what you really are.

Not so much man,
but a devoted Hanuman, serving god, cleverer
than the IBM, your demi-god.

Insignificance

The next time you start your car
do you call it a name?

The next time you go
for a walk do you call
it a name?

The next time you make
tea for a friend
do you call that act by a name?

The next time your dog
sneezes do you call that
a name?
Sarah, Gopi, David, Susie are
all just the next
time.

The next time a new galaxy
forms will the Duchess
of York open it with a name?

The next time the Universe dies
will there be an obituary
in The Times?

Kundalini

Kundalini
blue serpent
laser-like
flashing

crashing through
seven lotuses. Pain
Is over.

Superstring

Like all Sagittarians
you have this uncanny way
of blurting out the truth
without knowing it.

Take this phallic Symbol of Shiva
whose unyielding, ever erect linga
holds you in a trance
enters even your dream
through that dark window of half sleep.

Space is emptiness, in a consuming pain
that sucks in the mushroom cloud
of the big bang prakriti's womb
that procreates from the spores
of a primal explosion.

You compare the mushroom
to a phallus little knowing
it's spores like Shiva
form our reality first
ancestors, the nucleus
of the self, cosmic
source - little atom
that grew like a grapefruit
into a universe
physcists or super
computers still can't grasp.

Taurus

Why bull
this sly smile
as you crowd into the chinashop
of anther's proud contentment -
while jealously you guard your own
patch of green,
brook no intervention?

Your pretensions to gentleness
have gone.
The bull is out
in its true colour
mixing business with pleasure.

Weren't you in the courts of Greece
(ruled likewise by Taurus)
playing at sophistry? Clever you -
never caught on the horns
of your own dilemma - for the lack
of commitment to any creed
other than your singular,
well articulated need for pleasure
saves you the pain of straight talk.
Nothing vicious, nothing vile
but continuous, easy, pleasurable living -
who can blame that?

In the new age as
aquarius comes up for air
you watch safely
from the land,
the new exploiter - with a solid
pragmatic sounding charm.
You pretend
to blend work with leisure
when all you intend
is that others are goaded on
while you watch the fight
with detached pleasure.

At a Carnatic Music Concert in Madras

Synthesis of sound
by ancient men who
interacted with nature,
restructured molecules from elements and
stringing voices from the land
channelised them into music.
Unveiling vast universes,
infinities of space
within the haze of our being.

Look! Even the insomniac's eyes
are closing. Palms reflecting rhythm
and reaching for completion. These are
tuftless heads now swaying.

Bare walls of Vani Mahal, Madras
come alive as carved stone
as music covers her lovers like a blanket.
Rain-starred Madras
is fresh with jasmine.
This dusk is perpetual.

Diamonds flash like petromax lamps
on fair noses of women moving
from one marriage pandal to the next.
Thus the children and the nephews keep leaving
the calendar page where their stars were once marked.
Only this music, like the sacred thread
remains
to redress balance
with the ritual of age.

The Breath of the Shining Skull
for the Yogi and the Railway Buff

Father built this railway forty years ago.
As the train chugs up onto the wide mountains its steam engine,
like an ageing heart, struggles valiantly, missing a puff or two.
From the vantage point of the last cabin,
the Chairman's saloon,
he explains how we could measure the speed
of the train by counting the track beat,
rather like taking the pulse of an old sherpa climbing a mountain.
At ten, I had no guilt at the comfort of the saloon,
which, with three bedrooms and more
can accommodate three hundred others
travelling on the roof of the next compartment.

The train snakes up along its mountain tracks
and into a tunnel over two miles long-
time for an amorous but shy couple in the third class
to steal a quick kiss unseen in the dark
by prying eyes intrusive in the light.
Half an hour in the dark and the train emerges
into the blazing afternoon and steams,
stationary, on Punalur platform
where red bananas from the mountains
are seen for the first time in the journey.

The yogi calls it Kapala Bhasthi
the breath of the Shining Skull.
Like the train he puffs out hard,
each outward breath cleansing the sinuses.

After the cleansing he ejects
the steam of the 15 lettered mantra into the kundalini
and pushes it along the track to
the snow crested peak of Mount Meru,
the spine of the universe. Though still,
in the lotus mudra he moves upwards.

At the level of the throat chakra
the kundalini rests before its final ascent
into the most difficult tunnel,
where Shiva and Shakti embrace
after a cosmic day's separation.
Each speck of phlegm,
the smug ego of kapha and self orientation perish
in the exhaustion of the fight against base nature.

There in the light of the third eye, Shiva,
Parameshwara smiles. Vishnu -
maya burns inside and outside of him.
The skulls keep piling up.

Father was Parameshwar. But it is I, the son,
who now weaves the garlands
of skulls.

R.E.M.

God's sleep is the dream
of our existence. Neurons
of his dream crackle
an explosion of galaxies.
The birth of life is imminent, in
the next rapid eye movement.

In his dark body, as he sleeps
I see a white lotus creeping up
from the right atrium
into the throat.

He should soon awake, glowing
in pure consciousness.

My dream will cease.

Gemini London

Ruled by triple Gemini
this patch of London has largely been a haven
of peace, where the ravages of the world have not yet reached.

Even on a dark winter day the clouds
over the Nash terraces are kind
to the buildings. They frame the sky
with bright columns like
an old master's painting of mythical clouds
over the Greek archipelago. The park is serene
as the end of a journey to some remote hill
where there is no more strife.

London has been kind to us too.

Our ideas have taken shape and become active here.
The Geminian city breaks the Aquarian age's water
and like a child forces the world
to rethink old prejudices. It captures
imagination and space even as it crawls to the millennium
where the down turned head of London meets the river
like an Inca God's descent
into the Muladhara of the world,
exploding the dome.

The blitz once cratered these Nash terraces
and cleansed the city's soul.
The blitz to be soon launched from here
should soon cleanse the western soul.

The Philosophy of the Googly

The English, not good at philosophy
invented cricket, ultimate
example as game of how God intervenes
in human life. Even the untutored
can learn.

As the vedas say God comprises
of and commands five elements,
the Panchabhutha. All four
elements and the fifth, ether too
come completely into play on a cricket
pitch. The swing
for example, is dependent on and varies
with moisture and shine
on the ball and its speed in air,
whether the sky is overcast, in Sun.

Ether is the spirit without
which no team can win, the luck
of which hat to wear which seat to take
in the dressing room and what prayer
you say before you bat, what charm
you touch, what courage the press
and the crowd gives you to carry on
when we are all out for 162
and the other side is now 147 for 5.

Ganapathy Loves Cricket

Last Durga puja had a float with Ganapathy batting
and a little Krishna bowling a googly at the Lord of obstacles -
difficult to get out.

Pakistanis say their prayers and win
matches. Indians don't yet know
the Ganapathy trick WG would have gladly used.

Each time we had a match at school
I beseeched our cook or the driver
to break one coconut at the nearest temple for every
wicket I took. This arrangement worked well
and that season I averaged six
wickets a match bowling late
inswingers on dry summer days
unsuitable for a medium pacer
slower and more erratic than a Madras bus.

Then twenty years ago I left cricket
and chose a better game, not breaking them
but tenderly feeling softer ones placed attractively
on the anatomy of the weaker sex.
We longed for wicked maidens
not maiden wickets. That too was a fixture
in a cosmic cup of sorts.

Now I break coconuts for
Ganapathy in this final match to bowl Maya
out, tired after her long innings,
shuffling desparately at the crease.

Cricket at Lords

Living behind Lords
I don't have to be
at the grounds or watch T.V.
to know the score.

Each time there is grand
applause England has scored a four.
Polite applause is the opposition's
six. A deafening roar that shakes
the house is an Aussie wicket
or the L.B.W. of Tendulkar.
Pin-drop silence means England
wickets are falling like Ninepins

Last summer, by the lake in Regents Park
birds singing, world bright
and cheery I pass
a short, balding man in a fading three piece,
barrister's brief case underarm.
Perhaps an old Harrovian cricket fan.
He walks slowly, "a schoolboy with his satchel"
and a heavy heart.

On his boyish face is gloom.
The bright day
cannot touch his heart normally languid in the sun.

Obviously England has lost the Match.
Sadly I let him pass knowing his grief
but still long to commiserate
him for a sunny day
when all was perfect
except the score.

Priest Striding Towards Heathrow

My friend, the self preservative banker
always ashamed of his colour and Indianness
tells me disparagingly of a sight he saw
on the way to Heathrow with his American Banker friend.

From behind the driver's seat
the American's jaw drops open
at a vision on the M4.
He looks and sees

at 7am on a cold spring morning,
on the hard shoulder of the M4 a solitary Indian priest
brown skinned, bare chested,
sacred thread absorbing beads of sweat
in the early morning sun
striding towards Heathrow.
His head is half shaven with a tuft.
Under the red and vermillion caste mark
his eyes are deep and confident
intent only on his destination.
He is undaunted by the traffic,
the alien land or the white faces in the cars
that drive past him with amused stares.

His stride is long and purposeful.

Where is he walking to?

Is he taking a flight from Heathrow without his luggage?

Is he about to perform some powerful ritual in the heart
of heathen England?

Or is he himself taking off to Vaikunda
using the M4 as his runway
with a mantra on his lips?

Into Priesthood

for Francois Baumann

You had everything,
A degree from HEC, good connections,

charm. Was it the way
egotistical Oriel
left you for the schlumberger chap
that made you take
the final plunge?

Or was it the talk
of coming deluge?

In any case, Francois,
You were too good, too soft a boy for any single
girl to fully own.

Though I wonder
how you'll resist your fondness
for the steak tartare and winter
in Kitzbuhel.

HEC - Ecole des Hautes Etudes Commerciales - is France's Grande
Ecole for management studies.

Destruction of Tripura

From below mid-heaven he gazed, regretfully,
at the blue sky line shimmering
over the golden towers of the magical city.
Just two tears roll from his lustrous eyes onto his cheeks
in pity for those who do not
deserve his punishment, but the others
who are unfazed by the Gods, dared
challenge them and even their existence
must die. Their arrogance tilts
the balance of the cosmos.

The city's early warning systems are demonic priests
perpetually incantating mantras of the left handed
path. They sense his purpose and by their power
the city, like a vision in a crystal ball,
is made to disappear.

But only for a moment.
The Lord of the Dance is in no mood for games.
He opens his third eye only slightly and from between just two of its
lashes
emerges the nuclear beam to search and destroy.
The edges of the city are barbecued.

Then he raises his bow and releases the terrible
Aghora, the missile of doom for his enemies.
The city goes into flames and razed
to ashes falls like a burnt firecracker
into the abyss of space.
The souls of those who worship him
reach him as a little blister on his trigger finger.
The others, the evil ones, enter his bowel
as excreta of the cosmic one to remain
there until another kalpa.

That was a million years ago.

This is another time, another yuga.
Now there are over a thousand Tripuras puffed-up
with pride, their hollow leaders and media heroes manipulating
the minds of those who once worshipped him.

The king of them all bares his naked phallus to feminists seeking
conquest
of "their" ultimate linga and the fame
that goes with it when their own husbands' is chopped
off and thrown into the dustbin of contrived relationships.
In another city three murderesses are received
like queens and a queen is a murderess.
A hollow leader surrounds himself with
a kitchen cabinet of women, wearing high
heels to make himself taller. The domed ego of the millennium
must implode like the hollow
drums of their empty souls.

In this age of Kali it is Kalki who
bears the weapons of Shiva riding his faithful white
horse. From his tongue and his hands emerge the blazing
fires of Armageddon. Unlike Shiva
Kalki sheds no tears. His face has a thousand
masks. His weapons are secret. There is no early warning.
Save this.

He now takes aim.

PART IV

The Eternal

अहं ब्रह्मास्मि

I am the Brahman

After the Storm

People often ask me if I have
had a Guru or ever been
initiated. I then have
to say 'not really'.
Like the time, sensing the silence
in our house, some one asked if we had
children and I said the same, and my wife
laughed, "what do you mean - not really?"

It's true, though we have
no children, all who seek innocence
or childhood are children to the
world, hence to us.

I have never had a Guru but every fleeting act
of wisdom or compassion, intense flow
of love or even hate has taught me:
energy manifest in the weakest to the strongest
terrible form alone is Guru.
But, for me, energy has a distinct
form, a deity in tantric nature
in the lord of the Ganas -
Ganapathy -
manifest in strong
weak and neutral forms. The
Thamasic, Rajasic and Satwic
shades of man himself corresponds.

In positive, stronger form
he takes the shape of snowy
alpine peaks or the himalayan abode
of Rishis, the earth in pure
pristine form at the dawn
of Brahma's day. At that height he vibrates
in the lash of lightning synthesising vital protein.

He then moves
into prakriti, primordial
nature, slime, the abode of all
those who fell with Lucifer
when 'God' felt the pain,
the ecstasy of Creation, the separation
from his neutral state of Nirguna
parabrahman.

Over centuries
Ganapathy who inhabits the Mooladhara
in baser form begins to ascend
into his true abode,
a return to his mother, universal soul
at Sahasra Kamala.

Take this storm last night
a day before which the ivory
image of Ganapathy in Satwic form glowed
brilliant, fiery red and I prayed
"don't cause too much trouble
God". I am told instead
to focus breath in the eye
of the storm, suck it's energy
like mother's milk and say
a secret mantra with each heart
beat.

As the trees swayed
houses shook in fear
and the underground at Earl's Court
bellowed in anger
Your blue light appeared.
I wonder God in quelle quelle mode
you satisfy your hunger
for a little joke on this arrogant
species we proudly proclaim
near divine.

When Dido and Aeneas meet
fires do flash
The brash uncertainty of Pisces
gives way to humane Aquarius.
Elemental air commands the sea.
The earth must move.

Kaliyamardan

Just the dust from under your feet that drove
blue egoism from Kaliya
shower on me, Krishna,
kill this flowered serpent
curled around my head, Krishna.

Break this pot, Krishna
and when the sea
surges into the
stillborn void
I'll merge with you Krishna.

From Void

Stephen Hawking says Time lies
in the curvature of light into
another dimension.

The Hindus have always said that Time is in God's - Sree
Padmanabha's
exquisitively curved navel. In this lotus
junction, in the eternal singularity of void, upward,
and downward breath meet. Time and space begin

here, stalk growing into a time curve,
petals flowering as space.
God, even you, sweat around
the navel. From your navel's core, infinitely whorled,

emerge the beads of planetary illusion
like dew drops on a morning lotus.
Then, from the centre of a void, the Sun appears.

As the astrologers say, Atman, pure spirit,
making light
of the dewdrop's pretensions to self-hood.

The Marriage of Lord Venkateswara and Padmavati

This wayside temple in Domallur,
Bangalore, is peaceful and magical.
There is only the priest, a few devotees
and the dark granite stone warm
beneath one's feet.
The gentle breeze of a summer evening
carries the fragrance of jasmine
and Mysore's famed sandalwood.

The sculptures in panchaloha
of the God and the Goddess whose marriage
is being performed sit a few feet apart,
facing each other, dressed in the best silks
of Kancheevaram. The interaction between their hearts
is intense, almost audible.
Balaji looks intently at his bride to be, a half smile on his lips,
an experienced young lover, penetrating
her weaknesses, willing her into his embrace of love
and into union.

Poor Padmavati, princess as she is
cannot lose her noble reserve
knowing that if she looks
at him in his eyes she will become weak
and succumb to him like a schoolgirl, undignified
in the eyes of her friends who
drove him away as an unknown
suitor when he arrived on a white horse
just a few days ago. They would rather that
she was proud and showed off her royal lineage -
not so easily won over, jealous
that they may lose her for ever to this handsome lover.

But she does worse, not knowing where to look
and looking down instead with an aristocratic shyness
just above the platter of fruit in front of her
and seeming even more the willing victim
of his clever seduction.
(Sweet one, how unforgettably enchanting you looked).

....cont

She knows that later on she will be rebuked
by them for her meek and easy submission
to Vishnu, well-known bigamist.
(But Balaji is blameless here
having been asked to marry her by Sita
for saving her from Ravana as her shadow self).
Her parents will of course support her, knowing of
his promise to Sita, the Lord
having been described variously as a local lad
from the hills, a Prince
and as the ultimate Vishnu himself
who has condescended to marry their daughter
after a promise in his previous life as Rama
the destroyer of demons -
his purpose being the protection
of his devotees and the world
until the time for dissolution - when his third eye
merges with that of Shiva already playing
within him, half Goddess
other half caveman and renunciate.

Even the poor priest does not know
that padmavati's submission must be complete
before the marriage proceeds.

Though seemingly simply statues,
being imbued with divine life
the couple play their game
at the beck and call of their devotees
seeking prosperity, benediction or verisimilitude.
Biding time, until their devotees'
and their own Karmas are exhausted
and creation called back into the supreme self
like a complex theorem of trigonometry drawn
on the black board, proved and then wiped away
in divine boredom at the human ego and the taxing exactitude
of duality.

The Delhi-London Poetry Foundation

The Delhi London Poetry Foundation (DLPF) was set up in 1989 to promote poetry. Since then it has published a number of issues of the Delhi-London Poetry Quarterly (DLPQ), though not on a regular basis. The DLPF has also held poetry contests with over 5,000 poets taking part each time.

This is the first collection of poems published by the Foundation which is funded by a Charity from private sources and a small group of friends and well wishers.

DLPF is not commercially oriented. With the major publishers taking poetry off their lists, we welcome young poets who are interested in their work being published if they have an international, philosophical or mystical orientation.

"The Delhi London Poetry Quarterly is a most distinguished and beautifully produced periodical which is doing a great service to poetry" - *Sir Stephen Spender.*